the secret body language of girls

PORTICO

the secret body language of girls

Decoding the far-too-subtle Body Language of Women

mal croft &
matt windsor

First published in the United Kingdom in 2010 by
Portico Books
10 Southcombe Street
London
W14 0RA

An imprint of Anova Books Company Ltd

Design and Illustrations by Matt Windsor

ISBN 9781906032814

A CIP catalogue record for this book is available from the British Library.

10 9 8 7 6 5 4 3 2 1

Printed and bound in China by Imago

This book can be ordered direct from the publisher at www.anovabooks.com

Dedicated to stupid men everywhere

CONTENTS

Introduction

Secret body language of girls? Ha! I know what you're thinking. Girls are rubbish at keeping *anything* secret. And that's a fair point. They are. In fact, I'm not even sure why we've put 'secret' in the title – maybe it was just a devilish marketing ploy to make you think that this book contains information about women that had never been heard before, as if we had found out some weird secret devil gene or something.

We haven't.

This book basically just contains lots of pretty pictures and nice, big, juicy, entertaining swear words like FUCKITY and SHITBAGS that you wouldn't find anywhere near, say, a Jane Austen novel.

This book is not rewriting the rule book on Male/Female relationships. It's not reinventing the wheel in any way. It's not even trying to be big or clever. No, all this book has going for it is some very, very bad jokes and some clues about how to better understand a woman's ridiculous body language. Why body language I hear you ask? Because it's fucking hilarious, that's why. Think about it.

Throughout centuries, men and women, ladies and gentleman, bros and hoes, have been plagued by their differences and how ruddy complex each gender is to work out and decipher. Boys and Girls are completely bloody different in oh-so-many, many, many ways it's not funny. What is funny though is that the one single thing that unites the sexes together is the utterly stupid and freakish ways in which their bodies subconsciously try to communicate with one another.

The Secret Body Language of Girls is designed to teach you – a stupid male – the subtle hints and techniques to help you work out (and therefore manipulate!) if the girl of your dreams is either giving you the 'come on' or the 'jog on' across a busy room. By knowing these little 'visual signifiers', you can repress your usual male desperation to make a cock out of yourself and instead play it cool, stay calm and then turn on the sleazy charm.

Women, you see, have the ability to express their emotions in a verbal manner unlike men, but they can also express their innermost thoughts, secrets and desires through the subtle complexities of such bewildering and hypnotic actions as twisting their hair, licking their lips, touching their face, rubbing their neck ... hell, even scratching their knees is a potential sign of a girl's innermost intentions. DISCLAIMER: it may also mean she has itchy knees.

The old cliché that if a women fiddles with her hair when she talks to a man it means she likes him is just nonsense made up by men to make other men feel better about themselves. If a woman is playing with her hair while she is talking to a bloke it's usually because she wants to distract him from looking at her oversized rack, which he most definitely would have been staring at since the conversation began.

The art of studying body language relies on the human brain's ability to differentiate between the tiniest movement of a facial muscle or the slight gesture of a hand (even the subtlest stroke of a leg) and work out what it means. So many of the conversations between one another are silent and spoken through body language – as much as 30% – that the brain must work out what is being said without being able to hear any words. Whether it's a slight upper lip movement, a

lifting of a brow ever so slightly or a sudden clenching of the fist, the brain must detect, decipher and understand every move so to work out what action and response it must take.

Girls have developed such high skills of communicating body language that not only did a word like 'Whatever' become a full sentence and a statement of intent in its own right, the accompanying body language gesture also travelled the world as the flag bearer of how important modern day body language is, and how it is continually changing to keep up with the times.

Female body language, in particular, is more subtle and harder to study than males – they just seem to flail their hands about, gesturing crudely. Girls require more effort to decipher. Moreover, a woman will tease a man emotionally using her body, playing with him in some sordid, freaky social foreplay to see if he is a good mate and up to the challenge. Let's face it, you don't have that kind of time or patience – you're a man after all – you want the answers now, you want to cheat and could not give a fuck about verbal or non-verbal foreplay. You want the easy answers and don't care how you get them.

So here they are … in book form, with pictures, just the way you like it...

Tuck in!

FOR REFERENCE: Please see Cameron Diaz's dire 'The Penis Song' from her shit movie *The Sweetest Thing*.

Tiny willy

Ever since man woke up at the crack of Dawn, he has never quite understood the female species. Are they out to get us? Are they to be trusted? What's with all the cushions?

But the most important question on a bloke's lips is …does size matter?

The answer to that question, is, simply, *oh yeah*.

Think of it from this sexist's point of view – would a girl prefer a small piece of cake or a big piece of cake? Most girls would say a small piece of cake, just to appear polite and demure but the truth is they would really like the whole cake if possible and one fucking massive spoon.

Now, of course, size is relative. Big is fine. Medium is do-able. Small is just about workable. Baby dick? Well, that's just out of the question.

So, when you see a girl pull this expressive hand gesture – essentially taunting with her little finger – it means that a man with a Diddy P is nearby and that she wants her mates to know, perhaps to warn off other females in the bar from potential end-of-evening disappointment and/or to embarrass a guy socially if he is acting like a bit of a knob.

WHAT TO LOOK OUT FOR!

This is the ultimate male insult so don't be anywhere near it if you see it. Most 'nice' girls would do this behind a bloke's back so as to embarrass him socially (and get the message across) but not to his face, as that would make him want to kill himself. A bloke would much rather eat his own hands than be publically outed, in front of his mates no less, with Small Little-Man Syndrome.

I love you!

We all know human beings like to gesticulate with their hands when they talk. That's all body language is – a form of added expression – a way of emphasising your words further than your mouth and, let's be honest, very limited vocabulary can...

But this gesture is both rubbish and vomit-inducing – like texting 'MWAH' or 'LOL' or air kissing nineteen times per cheek. This overly-affectionate body language gesture, made in public to convey love and adoration to a man is just a cheap ploy to let other girls in the area know he is taken – so hands, and eyes, off!

It's often seen out and about when a newly involved couple can't bear to be away from each other for more than 10 seconds (a bathroom break, for example). In this scenario you may see a smitten, love-struck female initiate the gesture, followed by the blushing male partner looking around, embarrassed, before replicating it wimpishly. Cue much laughing and mockery from his mates who saw it and who will never let him live it down.

WHAT TO LOOK OUT FOR!

Normally occurs when a bloke goes to the toilet, mid-frenchy, leaving his girlfriend all on her own for a few minutes and already missing his tender kiss. The types of girl who do this are:

(1) Teenage girls who like Zac Efron and the Jonas Brothers.

(2) Love-sick psychos who would self-harm if you dumped them.

(3) Jealous girls securing their territory.

A bloke who is the intended recipient of this loving gesture is most likely to be highly embarrassed to do it back but feels compelled to accept it for fear of scorning his girlfriend. If you are a brave soul, why not laugh it off, muttering 'you must be fucking kidding me' as you walk to the loo. Or if you are not a brave man, as we suspect, just pretend you didn't see it.

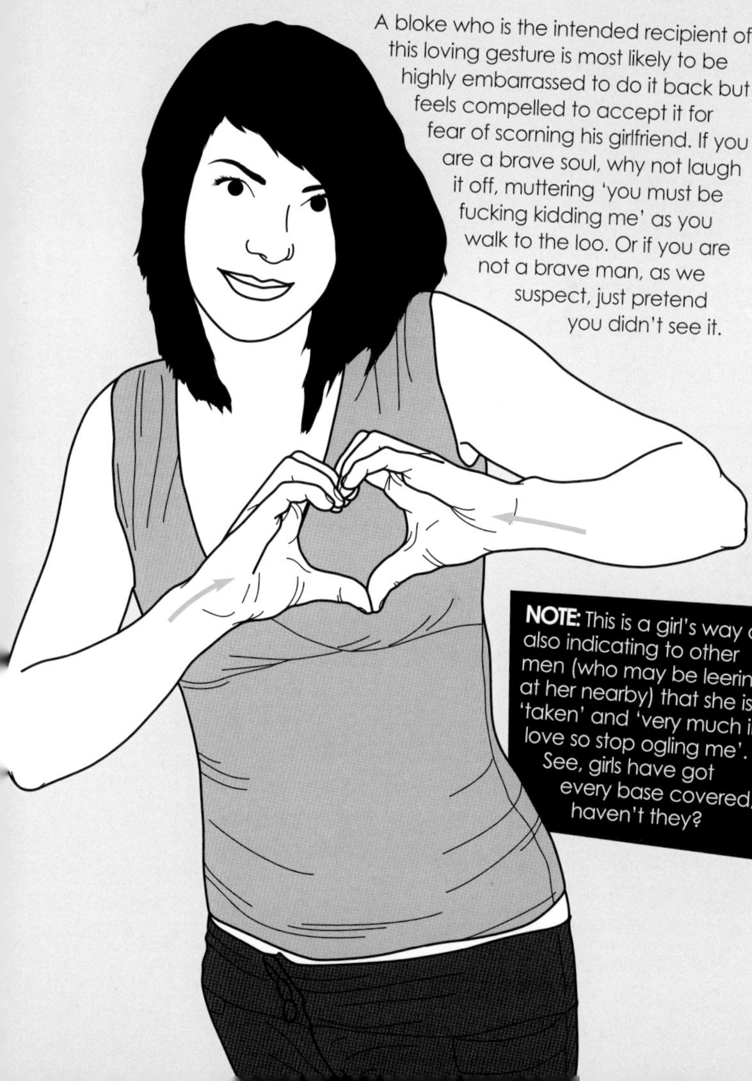

NOTE: This is a girl's way of also indicating to other men (who may be leering at her nearby) that she is 'taken' and 'very much in love so stop ogling me'. See, girls have got every base covered, haven't they?

Lip biting occurs most frequently at these three family occasions:

1) **Family weddings** (when she mentions the Bride's ex)
2) **Family Planning Clinics** (where she forgot to mention her ex) and
3) **Family Fortunes** (when she gets a answer wrong and gets an X)

Ooooops!
(or The Lip Bite)

Men know this 'tell' well. The Lip Bite is the female species' most universally acknowledged signal of 'Whoopsy Daisies' or 'Shit! I shouldn't have said that.'

To some men, the Lip Bite is a beloved, even cute, sign that a woman has made a small, minor mistake and is hoping no-one is going to notice. However, if this body language is followed by the phrase 'I think I just ran over the neighbour's son', then a much larger problem may have presented itself.

Many noted psychoanalysts believe that human beings bite their lips when they do something wrong as a way of inhibiting their mouths from admitting their mistakes publically – it's as if the brain's devious default setting is to keep schtum. Of course, no amount of lip biting is going to be enough, if you've just walked in on your girlfriend in bed with your brother.

WHAT TO LOOK OUT FOR!

The first sign of this mouth signalling is in the eyes. Do they dart around from side to side to see if anyone else has noticed? If so, chances are, the lip bite is next, followed by a 'SHIIIT!'. If your girlfriend is biting her lip, have a look around, what can you see?

(a) A dead person lying on the ground next to her?

(b) Your favourite vinyl record on the floor in a dozen pieces?

(c) The house, in the background, up in flames?

Not a chance!

Known in parts of Europe as the Brush Off, this thoroughly heartbreaking dismissal was created as a way of 'sweeping away' unwanted male attention without having to continuously repeat polite conversation where the end result was 'I'm sorry, you are just not my type'. Of course, what she really meant, but was too polite to say time and time again, was 'Fuck off, douche, not a chance'.

The Brush Off, then, was created by the sexy, savvy and popular girls that probably ignored you at school – the kind that all men desperately want to be seen talking to – to actively discourage blokes from approaching them. Any man who does, nowadays, just gets brushed away. All politeness is seen to be pointless in today's crude and chavvy society. Though most blokes think the Brush Off is a harsh way of being treated – and it is – it's no worse than how most blokes dismiss ugly women.

All in all, if you are a handsome man, you'll never be brushed off so unfairly (unless you have a personality like a dishcloth). However, if you are a very ugly man (and we assume you know this by now), prepare to be brushed away like a dishcloth with this horrifically humiliating gesture of smug superiority.

WHAT TO LOOK OUT FOR!

The Brush Off (so named because of the sweeping action made by the flick of the wrist) can be very discreet, as she probably can't even bring herself to look at you, so have your wits about you.

Have you ever been given the Brush Off in a really embarrassing way? Ever been told by a girl that you had more chance of getting a punch in the face than a look of her knickers? Send us your story, along with your name and address, and we'll print it and publicly humilate you!

Blokes are all too familiar with this body signal. It ranked Number 3 in the Most Annoying Female Body Language Signal Of All Time in a survey taken in 2007. Number One was, of course, 'Whatever', followed swiftly by 'Talk to the hand'.

Oh. no. you. didn't.

A familiar and unbearable form of expression – used by annoying females to indicate to other just-as-annoying females that what they just did should not have been done. While this is most frequently displayed between two females (usually before a cat fight), it has been known to be thrown in the direction of a male who has done something wrong and is just about to find out about it.

The Finger Wag, as we English have christened it, originated in African-American culture, seemingly in the past ten years, and has spread like wildfire to the UK as easily as, well, wildfire. Used predominantly as an aggressive communication to intonate personal power, authority and arrogance, the gesture is usually followed by a swaggering circling of the head and a pout to end all pouts. If you witness this hand and body signal in motion, chances are either a fight or argument is going to break out and somebody's eyes are about to be clawed.

WHAT TO LOOK OUT FOR!

If this happens to you, you're in for a difficult night, but to avoid that, look out for these body signals:

(1) Is a finger being waved in your direction? If so, which finger? You could be being told you have a small penis. *See p16.*

(2) Do you see a female shaped like a teapot with a spout?

(3) Do you sense major attitude bearing down on you?

(4) Have people suddenly started to move away?

(5) Are you starting to hear the sentence 'OH.NO.YOU.DIDNT.'?

(6) If so, remain calm, take it like a man and run away.

Watch me get served first

One of the most annoying things about body language is that woman can use it to their advantage, whereas most women see right through a bloke when he tries to do the same.

The female sex has a unique gift for using their body language skills on a man to get the things that they want without having to ask directly or wait – whether it's a drink at a bar, help with her workload or someone to tell a little white lie to the police about benefit fraud – men will always give in to a woman who knows how to use her feminine wiles. It's nature at its most unfair. Admit it, you've been duped many times before.

Normally, most men don't mind being taken advantage of in such pleasant and distracting ways, but it can grate after the tenth woman in a row has just used it for the third time. Especially if you are dying for a drink at a bar and just want the barman to recognise you rather than the umpteenth pair of tits he's been sinking his eyes into.

WHAT TO LOOK FOR?

If you have been waiting at a bar for quite some time, chances are it's because the male barman is serving the cleavages first. To beat the crowds, take the following action:

(1) 'Accidentally' trip up women on the way to the bar if they are going to get there before you.

(2) Signal to the bouncer that you suspect the girls in the queue were all just doing blow in the toilet.

(3) Ask the DJ to put Chesney Hawkes on repeat for half an hour and watch the girls flock to the dancefloor.

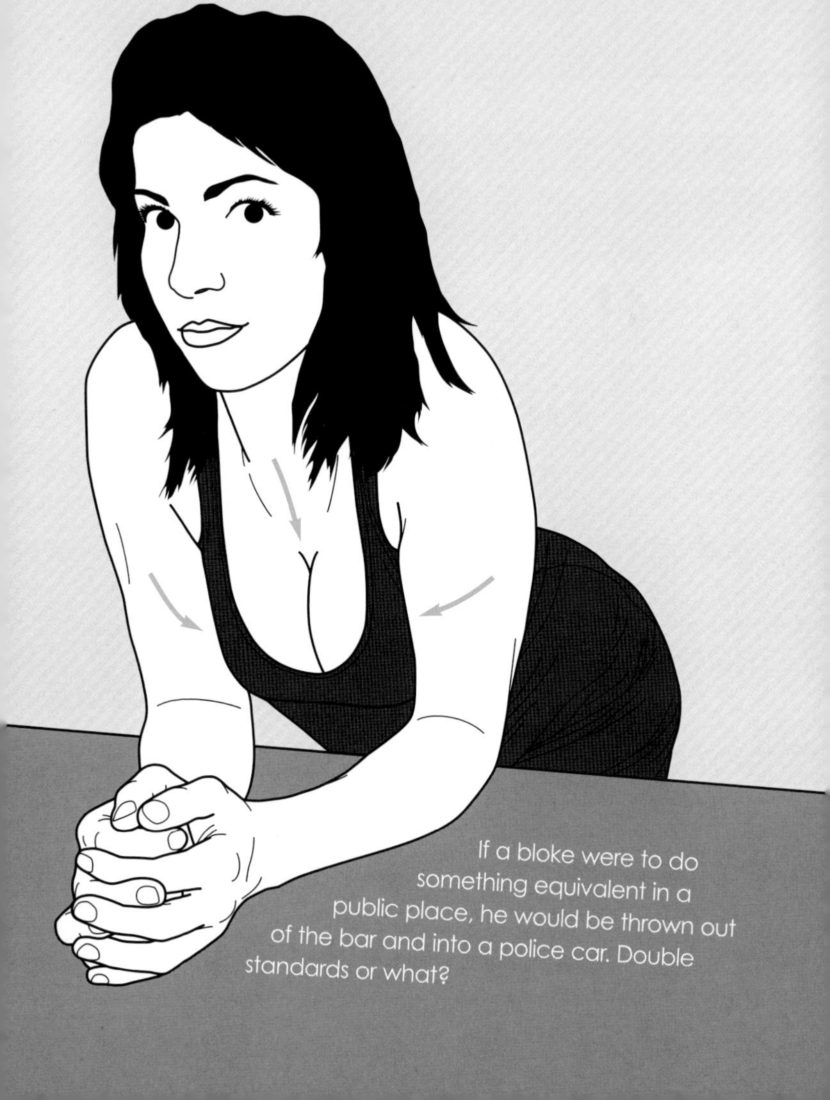

If a bloke were to do something equivalent in a public place, he would be thrown out of the bar and into a police car. Double standards or what?

Even some blokes have started to do MWAH now, not with other men of course, but when greeting female colleagues, female friends or new acquaintances. It has been absorbed by modern metrosexual man, where 'fake sincerity' is common place – the flaccid handshake is the perfect example..

DID YOU KNOW?
MWAH stands for…
Mummy **W**ants **A** **H**ug
and, supposedly originated in the 1940s when a mother would require an embrace with her grown up children after having not seen them in a long while. We did just make this up, but it sounds half plausible, doesn't it?

MWAH!

Ah yes, the fake air-kiss-noise-thing – the least sincere body gesture in the whole female canon of body language. So beloved by women around the world that they have forgotten just how entirely stupid it looks, feels, sounds and comes across to other people.

Not unlike the sturdy male handshake, the 'MWAH' feels laborious and unfriendly – as if you have a phobia of greeting people – and that irritating 'mwah!' sound (it's not even a real kiss, it's a noise designed to sound like a kiss!) just feels all wrong. Can you imagine a group of blokes doing it?

Apart from the stupid noise, and the fact that you don't actually kiss the person's cheek (you sort of kiss the air adjacent to it) the whole body signal looks uncomfortable – even though it was designed to reflect closeness and intimacy between the two people.

All in all, a joyless experience.

WHAT TO LOOK OUT FOR!

If you are about to be MWAH-ed to death, don't fear, look out for these defining features and try and escape:

(1)A woman approaching with extreme velocity shouting 'dahling!'

(2) If a woman is just pretending to like you, your cheeks will be about 3 miles apart when you 'kiss'.

(3) Does she prolong the 'mwaaaaah' sound out for a few more seconds than necessary?

(4) How many times do you kiss per cheek – 2/3/4/5? Once is enough surely? More than once and you will be MWAH-ed for life.

It was *this* big!

Infamous amongst lying fishermen and females around the planet, this cracking piece of unsubtle and inappropriate body language is easy to spot in a crowded environment – perfect for any bloke intent on listening in on girls' muck-riddled conversations from afar. If you see a girl displaying this gesture, you know they are not talking about handbags.

The polar opposite to a girl's use of body language for a tiny willy (see page 18), this exaggerated expression of a man's large, and obviously appealing, appendage wonderfully demonstrates the modern ways a female uses body language to articulate and express her liberated sexual emotions.

Unlike fishermen who exaggerate this hand gesture every time they tell someone the size of the fish they just caught, a girl will use this signal to accurately express the true length of a male's tackle, or rod (or whatever fishing metaphor you want to employ). The size should not change with each retelling. If it does, she might be a fisherwoman.

WHAT TO LOOK OUT FOR!

A girl performing this gesture to her friends is either showing off her latest man-quest or setting someone straight. Here are the signs to look out for in order to tell whether she enjoyed the experience...

(1) How wide apart are her hands? Wider than her own waist? Surely not? (2) Is she smiling or looking horrified? If the latter, chances are it was not a experience she'd be keen to repeat. In which case, you are OK. Go over and chat to her.

This hand language became famous (much to man's horror/pleasure), after slutty Samantha from *Sex and the City* used it, along with graphic language, to describe her latest conquest. This character became responsible for liberating the fantasies, thoughts and sex drives of a whole new generation of modern women. Men just stood by and smiled (though they would never admit to watching the show themselves).

WATCH OUT!

You may see girls use this body language on the dancefloor, as it does resemble the opening move to the dance 'Big Fish, Little Fish, Cardboard Box' that became popular in the 1990s.

If you are going to break out the Loser Sign, make sure you do it right, and be careful not to poke your eye out.

What a loser!

This is the most popular and most frequently used body language gesture of the modern era. Both sexes use it as an insult and it sprung to prominence in the 1990s, when Generation X took hold and its defining features – indifference, slacking and angst – could most easily be articulated through expressionless body language like shrugging, moping and looking bloody miserable. Indeed, a generation of teenagers became so apathetic, disinterested and unresponsive that the wild self-expression of the 1960s disappeared altogether. Kids of the 90s, through the 'grunge' music they listened to, expressed themselves more inwardly.

Nonetheless, one gesture prospered – The Loser sign. If counterculture and Generation X had a phrase or a defining signal then the Loser Sign is it. It expertly sums up emotions and this bit of body language, both unsubtle and lazy, easily conveys one's scathing intent.

WHAT TO LOOK OUT FOR!

Teenage female Generation X-ers are now referred to as Emos or Goths. You'll see this body language on High Streets on Saturdays outside HMV so watch out particularly for:

(1) Some shifty-looking female teenager looking all miserable and angsty (2) Probably a goth – check for dark eyeliner, jet-black hair and sarcastic attitude (3) Bad body posture (4) Use of language such as 'yeah whatever', 'OH.MY.GOD' and 'Don't be a loser, you loser'.

Whatever!

Most commonly associated with bitchy 'Valley' girls – normally so acutely observed in great comedies like *American Pie* – the hand gesture of 'Whatever!' is both annoying and brilliant at the same time.

A nonverbal communication designed to emote the female addresser's indifference towards a certain event, situation or person is probably the most common dismissal in the English language. This infamous hand signal – the forming of a 'W' with two hands – can cause tension and anger in the recipient who may, one day, reach out and snap off those accusatory forefingers and throw them in the river for the swans.

While most adults grow out of using this hand gesture, some bitchy females and gossip queens may hold on to it a bit longer because, as an argument killer, it does leave the person on the other end of it utterly speechless. And 'Don't "whatever" me!' is a pretty lame retort, isn't it?

WHAT TO LOOK OUT FOR!

If you are having an argument with your girlfriend and you can tell she is getting ready to unleash 'Whatever' as the basic response to your questions, then why don't you begin the argument by clearly stating that for every time the gesture 'whatever' is used during the argument, it means you're allowed to have sex with another one of her friends. Works every time!

While the signal 'Whatever' was famous in the 1990s, in the noughties, text-messaging speak has meant that the phrasing has been abbreviated to 'whatevs' used by chavs (both male and female) who are too sodding lazy to add one more syllable to their vocabulary.

WATCH OUT!

Really bitchy girls have even worked out a triple combination insult – the **Whatever Major Loser**. This can be achieved by turning the 'Whatever' hand signal upside down (to form the M for Major), then pushing the hand underneath to point towards the chest to form the Loser Signal (see previous page) in one swift action. Pretty nifty. Try it out!

If you find yourself in this situation, the best thing you can do is ask if your girlfriend would like a foot rub, a back rub, a hand rub and an all over body massage. If she's faking her headache she'll say 'yes' because she doesn't have to do any of the work, but yet is not too tired for some attention. If she says no, she's genuinely ill. Well, at least that's what we've worked out, and we are the experts (supposedly).

Not tonight love!

The three little words, along with 'I Love You', that bring the average bloke to tears – and not the good old-fashioned joyful tears that people enjoy, no, the crap version of tears that make men sad, depressed and frustrated.

'Not Tonight Love', accompanied by the usual faux temple-squeeze, is known to blokes throughout the land as the sign that there is no room at the inn for Little Jesus.

Women started using this not-so-secret body language in the early 1900s when they first realised that sex with men everyday can actually become quite boring, a bit uncomfortable and rather hard work if not in the amorous mood. They needed a get-out clause, a dismissive but courteous phrase that didn't hurt the feelings of the male lover but at the same time was strong enough to prevent pestering from a persistent partner.

So, they invented the fake headache.

And it worked.

For decades, 'Not tonight love' has become the get-out-of-sex card for women who, quite frankly, just didn't fancy being mounted by an ape like you at that particular moment. You see, for a woman, sex is all about the mood. For men, sex is, well, all about the sex.

WHAT TO LOOK OUT FOR!

Notice any of these casual phrases as you prepare for bed and you won't be getting lucky: (1)'I'm sooooo tired' (2) 'It's been a looooooong day' (3) 'Do we have any ibuprofen?' (4) 'Can you fetch a bucket... you know, just in case'.

I thought i told you...!
(Or The Finger Wag)

A stunning use of female fingers in this particularly simple, expressive (and sometimes very aggressive) gesticulation.

No man alive has never been on the receiving end of this type of finger pointing at some time, whether they were in the right or not. Finger Blaming, as men call it, is just one of the many types of uses fingers have in body language. In fact, research shows that fingers are one of the most expressive parts of the human body without taking your pants off. Whether those digits are wagging, prodding, pointing, stabbing, wiggling, pinching, clawing, even drumming, whatever, from a girl's point of view they are a quick and easy way of telling the boyfriend off after he's done something stupid or unthoughtful.

WHAT TO LOOK OUT FOR!

If you see The Finger Wag, you have probably committed one (or more) of the following misdemeanours:

(1) Been brought home in a police car. Again.
(2) Come home late smelling of the pub. Again.
(3) Left the toilet seat up. Again.

DID YOU KNOW?

The logic behind people crossing their fingers in times of uncertainty is because it indicates hope. To some people, crossed fingers look like a crucifix. Really?

In 2008 the word 'meh' (an interjection, in case you were about to ask) made it into the English dictionary beating off (oi oi!) 'huggles', 'frenemy' and 'jargonaut'. The origin of the word remains shrouded in mystery, though scientists believe it could have mutated from 'bleugh'. Possibly.

I don't care
(Otherwise known as the 'Meh' Response)

Female teenagers (and any women who just like to get in a huff for no reason), call upon the power of the 'Meh' to express themselves, even if the body language they give off is absolutely bone dry of any coherent articulation. Which helps.

As a bloke, you've probably seen this gesture countless times before, perhaps from a stroppy sister, a nagging partner or a female colleague after a particular intense meeting about her work standard or lack thereof. The dismissive scrunching up of the upper chest and expression of folded hands gives the recipient the indication that they just don't care what comes next out of your mouth – attitude literally dripping off their body.

The 'Meh' Response is also commonly seen by chavvy kids who have just received an ASBO after beating up a granny for her loose change. And that's fair enough, really, because let's face it, ASBOs are bloody pointless.

WHAT TO LOOK OUT FOR!

(1) A disgruntled female who didn't get her way.

(2) An upset female who will make sure you know she didn't get her own way.

(3) A female who has that look in her eye that suggests she will make your life hell for the next 24hrs because she didn't get her way.

Minger!

Just as blokes can be cruel about a woman's looks, a woman can be just as cruel (and as unsubtle) about a bloke's. Look around any pub, bar, restaurant, club, disco, and you'll see girls eyeing up blokes and blokes checking out girls – it's the done thing in the modern age (more so if you're wearing sunglasses) – but what you don't see is the response a girl makes after she's checked a bloke out. If you are good looking, she may mentally go 'phwoar' and stare at you until she has undressed you so much with her eyes you may as well be standing in your socks. If you are deeply unpleasant to look at, then the following bit of body language may come as no surprise to you…

Gagging, or retching, as it is sometimes referred to, is a common response to a chat-up line if you are ugly. The Brush Off usually follows swiftly.

Again proving that fingers are an integral part of a woman's body language signalling even if they are halfway down her throat. If you see a girl performing this action, don't feel sad, I bet your personality is amazing.

WHAT TO LOOK OUT FOR!

(1) A girl checking you out, then turning away suddenly with a look of horror.

(2) A girl with her fingers down her throat. Obviously.

If you are particularly or even violently unattractive, a girl may gag without the use of her fingers. This isn't body language so much as an involuntary reflex.

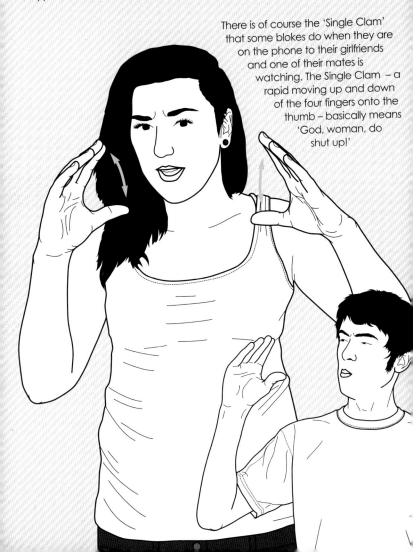

There is of course the 'Single Clam' that some blokes do when they are on the phone to their girlfriends and one of their mates is watching. The Single Clam – a rapid moving up and down of the four fingers onto the thumb – basically means 'God, woman, do shut up!'

Yeah, yeah...you're talking shit!

The 'Double Clam' has become synonymous, recently anyway, with chavs and council estate hoodlums. Of which, I hope you are not one. Though if you are, I bet you've stolen this book and not purchased it legally and you only did so because of all the funny pictures and big swear words like FUCK OFF that we've deliberately used to appeal to your type.

Anyway, this hand gesture has become a favourite in the last decade as a way of ordering, somewhat unpleasantly, the person you are in conversation with to shut the hell up. Like 'Whatever' and 'Talk to the hand', the 'Double Clam' is a dismissive gesture that uses the hands to infer a closing of the mouth. Of course, if you leant over and tried to actually shut that person's mouth with your hands it would be considered very rude. That's why body language is great – you can achieve the desired effect without having to use physical force!

WHAT TO LOOK OUT FOR!

(1) Any flapping of the hands is never good. Either someone is in trouble and needs rescuing or someone is talking way too much and needs to shut it.

(2) Establish if a woman is talking to another woman...if she is, she could be bored. Or fidgety. If the girl is doing it to you, because you've just spurted out some bollocks, then chances are she sees through your lies.

Sssssssshhhhhhhhhhh! (The Shush)

Every male knows The Shush. Every man alive has been shushed. If a girl shushes you then chances are she would have shushed you like this…it's annoying, right?

The Shush dates back to the Garden of Eden when Adam kept telling Eve to stop picking poisonous fruit from the Tree of Knowledge, because she'd listened to a devious talking snake. As if she needed telling twice, Eve's response to Adam was always 'Shush' as she took a big bite into a juicy apple full of sin. If only she had told the snake to 'shush', we'd all still be walking round naked, eating fruit and having a jolly good time with God. But we are not.

Since then, girls have been shushing men daily. The origin of the 'shush', as an interjection, derives from the word 'hush', but some clever clogs decided to put a 's' on the front of it and all of a sudden it becomes an onomatopoeic device loathed by the male form.

WHAT TO LOOK OUT FOR!

The Shush gesture is simple – the lifting of the forefinger to the lips. You are the victim of shushing in these situations:

(1) A woman wanting to watch the new Hugh Grant movie.

(2)A frustrated woman looking fed up at just the sound of your voice after you've been talking about some new type of spanner or surround-sound stereo system you've just bought.

3) You are still talking long after the woman has stopped listening and your voice has started to grate on her eardrums.

If libraries the world over collected all the energy expelled from angry librarians telling students to shut up, it would power Swindon for one whole hour. The Shush, then, is a powerful signal of expression, a universally acknowledged gesture of intent and a bloody annoying bit of body language.

NOTE

The shush comes in two forms:

(1) **The short stop** – 'Sh'. Used aggressively to make you stop talking immediately.

(2) **The long gasp** – 'Sssshhhhhhhh!. Used passive/aggressively to make you shut up, but in a nice way.

Obviously not all girls are liberated enough to perform this man-oeuvre in public places. The irony is that any girl you see doing this is probably a bit of a slag, and hence best avoided.

Come here

I swear to God we are not making this one up – this is an actual body language expression by which ladies signal to men that they are in dire need of copulation. In overtly sexual ladies, perhaps when they are at their most sexually potent (or just in need of a good seeing-to), a lady will gesticulate towards her nether regions to let nearby men know that she is available and that her legs are open to suggestions.

Most frequently seen in bars, between two flirting (and consenting) adults, the female will use this body language to coax a male to pay attention to her most fanciful parts. If he's a smart male he'll ignore it and play hard to get, but he's not so he'll fall for it hook, line and sinker. Based on the Aboriginal hand gesture of a 'V' to mean a lady's front bottom – as opposed to 'A', which would indicate a man's, er, front bottom.

WHAT TO LOOK OUT FOR!

If you see a girl 'displaying' (as they call it in the wild) then she is quite clearly in 'heat' and looking for a 'roger'. It's human nature and our advice is to get stuck in there quick. Not literally, of course...

(1) Is there a girl flapping her hands about nearby?

(2) Is she pointing in the direction of her, you know…?

(3) Is she looking at you with come hither eyes, snorting like a beast ready to charge?

I'm up HERE!

Eye contact is the most important thing to a girl. Even scientists agree. Eyes are the first port of call for any woman when they first notice a man – followed by the shape of the mouth and then the nose (oddly). One of the contradictions of modern life is that certain blokes seem to think that the first things women dig about them are their tattoos and gold sovereigns, and to some girls, they are. However, to girls not from Chatham, all the detail a woman needs to sum up a bloke is in his eyes. This is Flirting 101. If only men were to understand and reciprocate this simple action then everyone would be getting laid.

For blokes however, and you can see where we are going with this, the first thing they tend to notice about a woman is her chest – the concentrated area where all the boobage hangs around. There's no point in denying it mate. Blokes' eyes are drawn to them like plants leaning towards the sun, and while boobs aren't generally a good portrayal of female personality, they do go a long way towards deciding whether there will be a successful end to the evening.

WHAT TO LOOK OUT FOR!

(1) A guy looking at a woman's chest deep in conversation.
(2) A woman getting frustrated – though I bet she is wearing a skimpy top.
(3) The finger-wrist flick pointing from her breasts up to her head, indicating that said guy is looking in totally the wrong place for a meaningful conversation.

This classic finger-wrist gesture, designed by girls as a means to divert the male's attention from her chest – and into her eyes – became more common in 1990s when girls started wearing skimpier clothing, plunging necklines and push-up bras – giving guys absolutely no chance of being able to look anywhere else. Oh, the irony.

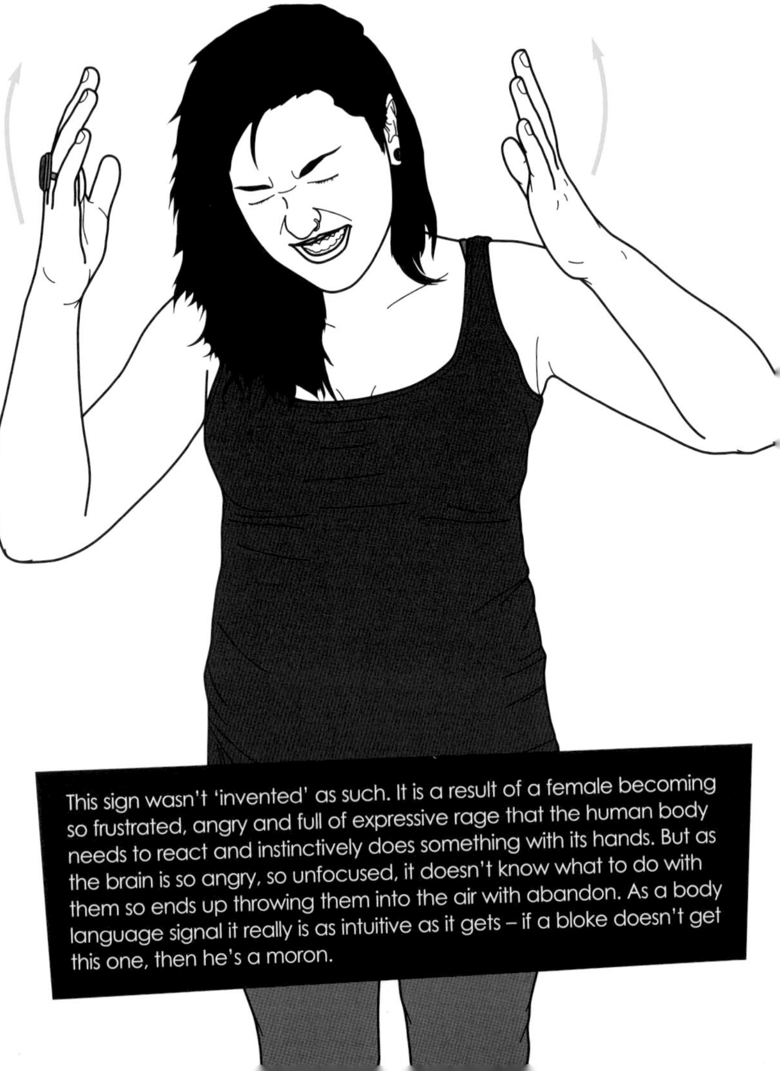

This sign wasn't 'invented' as such. It is a result of a female becoming so frustrated, angry and full of expressive rage that the human body needs to react and instinctively does something with its hands. But as the brain is so angry, so unfocused, it doesn't know what to do with them so ends up throwing them into the air with abandon. As a body language signal it really is as intuitive as it gets – if a bloke doesn't get this one, then he's a moron.

Useless!

The art of studying body language relies on the human brain to be able to detect the tiniest movement of a facial muscle or the slight gesture of a hand or even the subtlest stroke of a groin. So many of our conversations between one another are silent and spoken through body language (as much as 30%!) that the brain must work out what is being said without being able to hear any words. Whether it's a slight upper lip shift or a faint lifting of a brow, right through to a sudden clenching of the fist, the brain must detect, decipher and compute every move so that it can comprehend what each action means, no matter how subtle or casual it may seem to the other person.

Of course, that's all completely irrelevant when you see this body gesture occur. Definitely one of the most unsubtle, melodramatic and OTT gesticulations in the English (body) language, and one that girls use every day. But, let's be fair, that's because blokes are useless.

WHAT TO LOOK OUT FOR!

The dismissive throwing of the hands in the air – the classic signal that you've gone and buggered up again.

If you've screwed up, let her down or ejaculated prematurely you'll see your girlfriend, wife or fuck buddy (respectively) use this piece of body language. So, you've screwed up, big deal, here's three things to do to get back in her good books:

(1) Get out of her sight immediately.

(2) See (1).

(3) See (1) and (2).

Talk to the hand!
('cos the face ain't listening)

This intimidating body gesture rose to prominence in the 1990s, like most other smart-arsed things that thought they were funnier than they actually were (e.g. *Seinfeld*). The 1990s was the decade of the wise-ass – everyone thought they were a comedian. Whoever first said 'Talk to the Hand' probably thought it was fucking hysterical, but sadly, as we've learnt in the subsequent ten years, they were just the annoying douche who had given birth to one of the most irritating phrases and body language signals in the world…ever!

Girls of a certain age and demographic (i.e. chavs) will use this signal, principally an outstretched arm, as a way of getting other people to shut up because they are not interested in what they are saying. Of course, they could just say 'shut up' but that would be far too easy and not nearly as humiliating for the other person.

WHAT TO LOOK OUT FOR!

You know you've been the victim of this terrible body language crime when you see a girl outstretch her arm, and shove the palm of her hand into your face. Her face, at this point, will look like she's chewing on a bulldog's bumhole – full of attitude and insolence. If this happens, the best thing you can do is grab her hand and talk into it, as if it were a microphone, whispering 'Hello, er, yeah, can you tell the face to stop being such a dick?'. That will shut them up fast.

Some people have been known to respond to this intimidation with the rejoinder: 'Yeah, whatever... talk to the finger because the hand ain't listening'. Such mockery is just what this preposterous phrase deserves.

Bopping is the ultimate sign of drunken behaviour. Both blokes and girls are guilty of doing it to impress the opposite sex with their flexibility, rhythm and fun nature. Remember, for a girl, dancingl is serious business.

WARNING!
Bopping may induce feelings of embarrassment, shame and realisations of 'Jesus, how drunk was I?' the morning after.

I'm soooo drunk! (The Bop)

The 1970s has a lot to answer for. Not least because of its shitty fashion sense. In American politics, President Nixon was being the ultimate buzzkill after the high of the 1960s, a decade that effectively took the piss. In music though, the Americans were stealing all the limelight back from the British. How? With funk, and this snazzy little number, known among body language experts as Body Popping, or Bopping, for those of you who like portmanteaus.

Bopping, while a highly coordinated and popular dancefloor move – incorporated by dance choreographers the world over – is also at the mercy of every girl who after too many vodka lemonades (i.e. two) starts to think she is the next Britney Spears. The body pop is just one of a whole array of wildly chaotic, and plain bad, dance moves a girl will initiate on the dancefloor to display to the men around her that she is a dancing queen. This is exemplary body language flirting practised by girls to demonstrate to the blokes standing around the dancefloor, circling them like birds of prey, that they are drunk and looking for a possible fumble on the bus home.

WHAT TO LOOK OUT FOR!

(1) A girl's hair flailing about all over the show.
(2) The look of deep concentration on the girl's face – as if mastering this move is the only thing in her life that matters right now.
(3) Aggressive pelvic thrusting.

Hottie alert!

Attractive blokes are hard to come by these days – or so women claim. The invention of super-strength lagers, Playstations and the internet have made modern men a more gruesome, ugly and socially inept bunch of smelly old arses than ever before in the history of the Male species.

Some researchers believe that Modern Man has reverted back to his Neanderthal ways (after 30,000 years of inventive flourishing), since now that everything has been invented, we can sit on the sofa again with some oven chips and relax. Good news for men, bad news for the ladies. With men becoming uglier, women are resorting to overreacting when they see a hot guy walk by – as if they suddenly lose all control of their dignity and grace. This overreaction is a body language gesture deliberately designed to show female friends that she immediately needs calming down. Perhaps with a cold compress and some smelling salts. Or the guy's phone number.

WHAT TO LOOK OUT FOR!

If you've just walked past a girl, and she exhibits any of the following symptoms, turn around quickly and make your introductions because she's just displayed clear signals as to how she feels about you.

These are the signs of your perceived hotness:

(1) A usually calm and collected female going into a blind panic. (2) A flapping of hands (3) Blushing (4) Swooning (a form of mild fainting from Jane Austen novels) (5) Stuttering – 'Hello, nice to meet you' becomes 'Pablo, mice to neat moo".

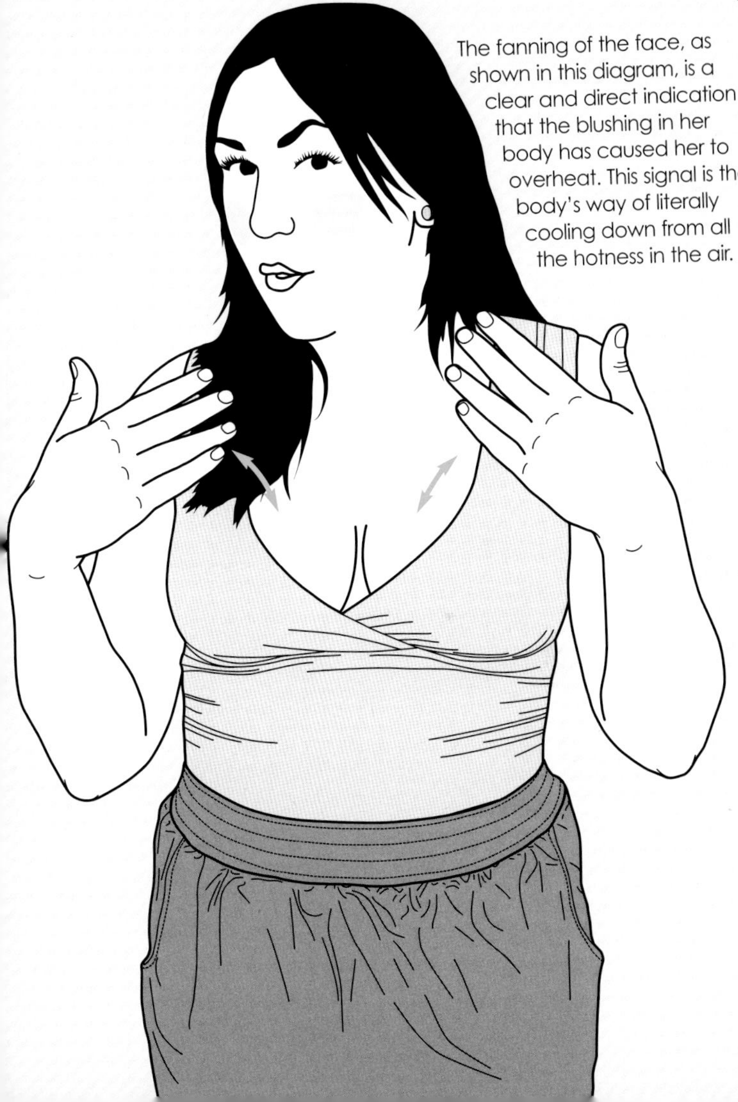

The fanning of the face, as shown in this diagram, is a clear and direct indication that the blushing in her body has caused her to overheat. This signal is the body's way of literally cooling down from all the hotness in the air.

The Eyes Have It!

How a girl's lying eyes can look like they are anything but...

The eyes, supposedly, are the window to a person's soul. But also the window to, er, a brain full of lies. When your girlfriend next moves her eyes, take notice, because what she is saying is perhaps not what she is thinking:

Straight up – I'm trying to think of an instantly believable lie **e.g.** *The car got scratched because some hoodies keyed it, not because I bashed the shopping trolley into it.*

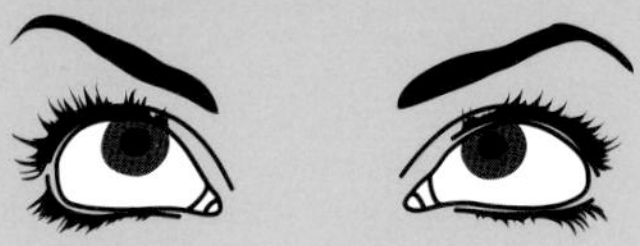

To the right and up – I'm trying to calculate how damaging the truth will be. **e.g.** *I once snogged your best mate when we were on a 'break' but never told you.*

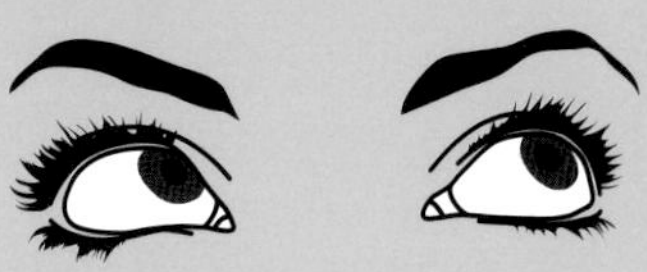

Straight down – I'm upset that you would think I am lying to you **e.g.** *I'm a shit liar and I know that you know that.*

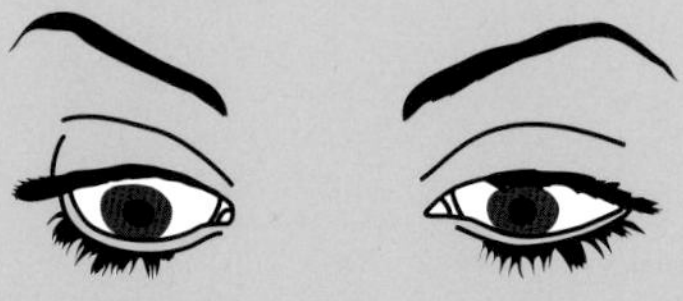

To the left and up – I am absolutely lying to death **e.g.** *I have never lied to you, I promise.*

Anticlockwise rotation – Typical Man! You never believe me!
e.g. *You always think I'm lying, when really you just want to think that so your male ego doesn't get bruised.*

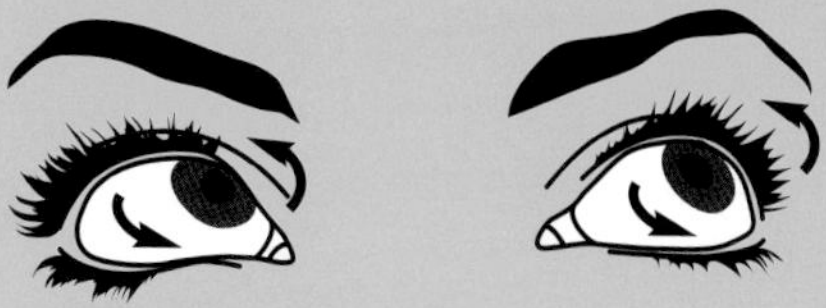

Air kisses
how many is too many?

OTT and pretentious air kissing has become the unwanted child of social etiquette. Nobody is sure how it happened or where it came from, but now it's just getting totally out of hand.

Where will it end?

One Kiss – strangers being polite.

Two Kisses – close friends being friendly.

Three Kisses – lovers in bed.

Four Kisses – only in France.

Five Kisses – For people with nothing better to do in the afternoon

The Fake Kiss – I hate you really, please fuck off and die.

"……………!" (air quoting)

Voted this year as the Most Annoying New Body Language gesture, air quoting has very swiftly become the most reviled gesture the hands can display without being either aggressive or insulting. Often used to indicate sarcasm or irony, air quoting – the virtual quotation marks when someone is speaking – makes anyone nearby want to snap off that person's fingers with the savagery normally reserved for a granny beater.

Popularised in the 1990s, the term 'air quoting' first appeared in 1989, but historians believe that smug idiots have actually been performing the hand gesture since as far back as 1927. Also referred to as 'Ersatz Quoting' due to the fingers 'imitating' the actions of the mouth, or sometimes 'bunny ears', but that's just stupid.

WHAT TO LOOK OUT FOR!

If you see a girl using air quotes it usually means she is saying one of the following three things:

(1) I don't care if your mates said it was "normal" … it's not, now go to the doctors!

(2) I can't believe you called my mother a "dirty old cow".

(3) Where is this "treat" you promised me then?

"While this hand gesture is not only used by girls, it does sum up the sarcastic attitudes some women adopt in arguments with their boyfriends. Whereas men just sulk, girls like to bring out the big guns – sarcasm and irony."

Men, as a rule, don't get mad if a girl comes home late pissed without pre-warning. In fact, they would prefer it every night. Not because they don't care, but because it gives them a chance to catch up with online Pro-Evo.

What time do you call this?!

A nose snort, folded arms, tense shoulders, a tapping foot, a bellowing voice – it can only mean one thing – you've fucked up again! Maybe you said you'd be home at 8pm and it's now 3.45am and you are completely wrecked and have lost a shoe. Maybe you said you'd phone her when you got there, but forgot. No matter what you did wrong (and you are clearly in the wrong) then expect to face this stony-faced piece of body language from the girl in your life. Whether it's an angry mother or a disappointed girlfriend (or both if you happen to live with them both) most blokes would expect to come home to this body language at least once a week. Like a steak dinner.

This type of body shrug accurately reflects a woman's ability to multi-task – the language is both defensive and aggressive all at the same time. A bloke doesn't know how to feel or react. It's the perfect body signal to let a man know she is both disappointed and pissed off all in one, the body language equivalent of how, if you had done something to upset your mum, she wouldn't get angry or upset, just silent. Which makes it even harder to bear.

WHAT TO LOOK OUT FOR!

You're in trouble. Face it. Here are three ways to blag out of it using your very own creative juices:

(1) Don't look at her in the eyes – they are like tractor beams at this point. If you do, she'll eye-screw the truth out of you.
(2) Tell her you'll buy her anything she wants to make it up.
(3) Go OTT with flattery and balls-out charm.

Tsk!

Men often refer to women, rather condescendingly, as 'bloody women!' after they have done or said something stupid, ridiculous or dangerous – be it a hilarious 'blonde moment' or, worse, mowing down a cyclist coming off the A34. This condescending remark, while politically incorrect, wonderfully sums up the differences of expression between the two sexes. Men, all aggressive and verbal, whereas women are more subtle and nonverbal – as seen in this affectionate, but no-less-condesending, body language – The Eye Roll.

The roll of the eyes, amongst girls, is one of the most familiar facial responses when a man has screwed up or, most commonly, gone all stubborn. Normally accompanied by the phrase 'Tsk! Men!', this body language can become quite grating after a while.

WHAT TO LOOK OUT FOR!

Don't panic men, you can see the Eye Roll coming from a mile off. If you do any of the following, expect the eye roll to follow immediately:

(1) You've got lost on the way to your friends' house-warming party. And then point-blank refused to ring them up and ask for directions.
(2) You've bought a new gadget, taken it out of the box and promptly broken it. And you refused to read the manual.
(3) You've forgotten your 5 year Anniversary. You've rushed out to buy flowers from the petrol station. Then left the price tag on.

See our special section on p60 to learn more about The Art of Eye Rolling.

Never ever tell a woman to 'calm down, dear', especially if you've just admitted to putting your red jumper in with a white wash. This will only further exacerbate things, and at this stage, you wouldn't want that.

I can't believe you did that!

Hell hath no fury like a woman scorned – so said William Congreve. And how bang on he was (whoever he was).

There are few things in life that put the fear of God into men, but a woman on a (argu)mental rampage is very high on the list – especially if you know you are in the wrong and there is nothing you can do or say to make the situation any better – you've just got to shrug your shoulders, get on your knees and admit defeat. Not that that helps. There aren't too many aggressive female gesticulations, the majority are more subtle, subdued and considered. However, if you have sent your missus into a blind rage because you left the baby in the pub, then be prepared to witness this truly horrifying display of emotions. Be afraid. Be very afraid.

WHAT TO LOOK OUT FOR!

So you are in trouble and the missus is about to kick off. Here, in ultra slow-mo, are the first five key things you'll notice:

(1) The face filling up with blood. This will give the face a certain amount of rosy-cheeked redness that you'll want to keep an eye on. The redder it gets, the further away you need to run (2) The arms tense up. The fists clench. The shoulders tighten. This is the first sign of her winding herself up, about to uncoil (3) Stomping up and down. This is her body's way of releasing anger in a way that isn't using her fists on you (4) Screaming at the floor. This is called venting. Don't interrupt (5) Pulling her hair out. This is the ultimate sign of frustration. Wow, you must have really messed up!

Is that weirdo still staring?

Chances are you'll never see a woman do this, purely because you'll be that weirdo the woman is indicating to her friends out of sight. But believe us, if you have ever spotted a beautiful-looking woman in a bar and then proceeded to stare at her all night, then this will have happened to you.

Blokes think that staring at a girl all night may be a good way of flattering her, by letting her know that he thinks she is beautiful and deserves his undivided attention, even if it is just the odd sly look in her general direction every couple of minutes. To a woman, this constant staring is just going to make her think he is a bit of a nutter. It's one of the biggest ironies in the history of dating. The more a man shows his enthusiastic interest in a girl, the more scared or put off the girl gets that he's a crazy stalker.

WHAT TO LOOK OUT FOR!

If you are being ignored by a good looking girl, don't worry, just join the back of the queue. However, before the bouncers come over and kick you because they've received 'a complaint', best to look out for these body language signals:

(1)She's turned her back on you.

(2) She's pretending to be on her phone when she walks to the loo, so you won't approach her.

(3) She's told her friends about you, and they have proceeded to give you the evils.

Call me!

As familiar to men as it is to women, the universal body language motion of 'call me!' is as shit and pointless today as it was thirty years ago when the mobile telephone was invented. Of course, back then the phone was the size of a large housebrick, hence why the hand gesture still uses the whole hand to demonstrate it. Nowadays, phones are the size of a funsize Mars bar and the body language has not moved with the times to reflect this. Because that would look even sillier.

The cries of 'CALL ME' from departing friends or new lovers can be heard all over cities around the world followed promptly by the man or woman sticking their hand pointlessly to their ear and then wiggling it around as if it was the International Sign Language for deaf people. Which it is.

WHAT TO LOOK OUT FOR!

On paper, a girl sticking her hand to her ears pretending it was a phone makes it seem like she was a bit mental. In practice, if a girl does it to you, great, it means she likes you and wants to call you. She wants to call you because of one, or maybe all five, of the following reasons (in order):

(1) 'You made me laugh'.
(2) 'You're cute'.
(3) 'You have kind eyes'.
(4) 'You are a lot of fun'.
(5) 'I have two weeks to live and you're the best I can get in such a short time frame'.

Gimme 5!

Adored around the world, the High Five is everybody's favourite way of gloating – be it a promotion at work, getting married or finding out your dead grandmother was loaded.

A celebratory gesture between two people, it supposedly originated in 1970s LA thanks to Glenn Burke – the head coach of the Los Angeles Dodgers. Though that's what Wikipedia says, so it's probably totally and woefully inaccurate.

There are many differing variations of a high five, some with different outcomes – the 'Air Five', the 'Too Slow', the 'Low Five' and the 'Back Hand Five'. All of these are just extensions of the same thing, probably invented by people with way too much time on their hands.

WHAT TO LOOK FOR!

At the end of the day, it's just two people slapping each other so let's not make a big fuss over it. When it comes to body language, however, this gesture is one of the biggies: If you see two women high-fiving, chances are one of them is:

(1) Pregnant.
(2) In possession of a winning scratchcard.
(3) In possession of some top drawer weed.
(4) Newly single after finally dumping her weed-dealer boyfriend.
(5) Walking into someone else Sieg-Heiling.

Also known as 'Giving skin', this expression of celebration has its own day – National High Five day – the third Thursday of every April. It's not quite a national holiday, but in the US particularly (well, exclusively) everybody greets each other with a high five, except for those who are 'too slow'.

For the pure and innocent, fellatio is not the name of your Croatian neighbour's cat. That's philacio. Fellatio is society's polite and scientific term for a blowjob. Different to 'Giving skin', but, when you break it down, it's the same thing.

Get in my mouth!

One of the newest examples of contemporary body language devised in the noughties, this is both graphic and crude, but then that's the modern woman for you. And if you don't believe us then go to Newcastle for a night out.

A group of girls, out on the town enjoying the sights, are sometimes seen to be doing this comic hand gesture to signify that a hot guy has walked past and wish to alert their friends to their intentions, and being the first thing they could think of, they mimic fellatio.

Now why this is the first thing that comes to their minds is a question you'd have to ask girls, but you would imagine it's for the more liberal, sexually uninhibited girls that have broken down society's prudish attitudes towards sex and just enjoy it as nature intended. And to be fair, blokes are twice as bad.

WHAT TO LOOK OUT FOR!

This body language action is exactly the same as what a girl would do if they wanted to be voluntarily sick – perhaps because they drunk too much or, say, after a really ugly guy has just walked past. You can see how this would be confusing to a guy, right? To make sure the woman is doing it because she thinks you are hot, rather than the unpleasant alternative, check for the following signs:

(1) Vomit isn't actually coming from her mouth.

(2) She continues to look at you in a nice way after you have walked passed.

(3) She may just be coughing. Keep staring to double check.

I'll facebook you!

Facebook has become the new myspace, myspace was the new email, email was the new phone call, the phone call was the new cave drawing etc etc etc...you get the picture.

As technology evolves so too does the communication of expression of human beings. Body language doesn't remain rigid in time, new body poses, postures and ways of articulating thought through the body are being invented all the time. Some people actually put a lot of thought into it. Not this one though...this body language signal is just a girl pointing to her 'face' then pretending to open a 'book'. It's fairly simple. Girls across noisy nightclubs or rowdy pubs are performing this action all over the country, upon departing from their friends, as a sign of their intention to contact them via facebook – the internet's newest and 'most popular social networking site'™.

WHAT TO LOOK OUT FOR!

Essentially, if you see a woman pointing to her face and then pretending to open a book, it means she'll facebook you and send a comunicay. As a lucky recipient of a message from a girl don't be surprised if she sends you one of the following confusing things:

(1)A poke.

(2) A wall post.

(3) A message.

(4) An invitation to play scrabulous.

(5) A small picture of a dog.

(6) 'Jenny is a princess...what type of fairy tale character are you?' – type questionnaires.

Did you know that facebook rape – the practice of hacking into someone's facebook account and sending out nasty messages to that person's friends – is called Frape. A facebook stalker, someone who stalks you on facebook is, sadly, not called a falker.

Fig. A

Fig. B

You can acknowledge a girl's hair-playing by looking at her hands as she does it or by holding eye contact with her. This will let her know that you are interested in her too. But, for God's sake, don't play with your hair as well. That's called 'mirroring' and will freak her out.

WARNING! If the girl you are chatting to is a hairdresser, be warned, she may only be playing with her hair out of routine and habit.

I like you a *lot!*

One of the oldest, and famous, 'protean' body language tells that exists. All blokes know if a girl plays with her hair while she is talking to him, she must like him a lot – it's like the worst kept secret in body language. To a boy, the girl might as well be wearing a T shirt with 'TAKE ME' written all over it.

Protean body language, named after The Proteus Effect – a Greek God who could 'shape shift' (yeah mate, whatever) – is the power of the 'tell' that precedes flirting. In this instance, the girl is preceding her flirting with a bloke by playing with her hair – a subconscious 'tell' that she fancies him as more than just a friend. Usually the playing of the hair consists of twisting a few strands of her hair by her eyes. If she really likes you, she'll be flailing her hair around melodramatically, tossing it every which way that is possible.

WHAT TO LOOK OUT FOR!

If a guy picks up on this tell, he should turn his charm dial up to eleven as he is onto a winner. Typically though, most guys don't pick up on it as they are too busy trying not to stare at the girl's chest. If the girl you are talking to has no hair, don't worry, she'll probably be doing a few of these other 'subtle' tells:

(1) Licking her lips (2) Stroking her neck (3) Touching your sides and arms gently (or knee, if sitting down) (4) Staring at your groin (5) Trying to hold eye contact with you (6) Eating a lollipop suggestively. This only applies if she has a lollipop upon her person. Make sure she is over eighteen.

What a nightmare!

When involved in an argument with a girl you know she'll display some fairly outlandish and melodramatic bits of body language just to really drive home the point of what an idiot you are being. These signals could range from the subtle (a clenched fist) right through to the OTT (pulling of hair). Somewhere in the middle you'll find this frustrated response – the tension in the face accurately reflecting her inner turmoil and the pointing to her temples being her brain's way of saying 'stop fucking with my mind!'.

WHAT TO LOOK OUT FOR!

This can be a fairly unpleasant thing to observe – the inner frustration of a girl about to explode doesn't make for pleasurable viewing, as spectacular as it is likely to be. Like the old saying goes, 'Fireworks are great to look at, but you wouldn't want to be near one.' To avoid seeing this body language do the following:

(1) Apologise profusely even if it wasn't your fault.

(2) Compliment her on the way she looks, even in the morning when she doesn't look so good.

(3) Make her feel like she is special – the only person in your life who understands you – even if you think, deep down, that bros should always come before hoes.

You'll also see this hand movement followed by the phrases (in order):

a) I've had enough
b) It's not working
c) My friends were right all along
d) Get your stuff
e) You're such a loser!

If you are going out with a girl, and know that her previous boyfriend was rich, or at least had more money to frivolously spend on her than you do, face it: the relationship is doomed. She'll want to be kept in the style to which she has become accustomed. **TOP TIP:** When it comes to money, girls, unlike Leeds Utd, don't relegate themselves downwards once they've experienced the Premier League. Remember this.

He's minted!

Gold-diggers – WAGs usually, or the fame-hungry girls who appear on *Big Brother* – love money. They like the smell of it, they love the taste of it (when it's pulped down and made into smoothies), they love the way it feels inside their clutch purses and they absolutely love the way it provides a security and happiness that men can rarely live up to. For these girls, money is the only thing they would be interested in you for.

So, if you're a bloke and you've got a bit of money – maybe inheritance, or you've won the lottery, or you are a banker stealing other people's money or you just work really hard – whatever – be careful not to hook up with any girls you see making this very unsubtle finger gesture because you won't be very rich for very much longer.

WHAT TO LOOK OUT FOR!

Gold-diggers make up approximately 1/5 of woman aged 18-50 in the UK so that's about 15 million women (hey, don't argue with statistics). Chances are you know one. Here's how to tell:

(1) Do her eyes light up when you mention the word 'cash'?
(2) Does she talk about all the exciting things she did with her last wealthy boyfriend?
(3) Does she say the word 'Darling' or 'DAAAHLING'?
(4) Does she start panting whenever you approach a hole-in-the-wall?
(5) Does she doodle '£' signs when she's bored?

Look into my eyes!

Forget all these wildly melodramatic body language signals for a minute. Eye contact is what matters most as it provides most of the emotional information women need to make a decision about a guy – plus, from the brain's perspective, it's the easiest nonverbal communication to develop with the greatest reward – a *connection*. It's also the key to a door that blokes may not be quite ready to open too early in a relationship. A woman will want to look into a guy's eyes from the first date – get a feeling what kind of person he is – but a man may find this level of intimacy too much too soon. He'd prefer to keep things at a distance until he's sure that she means more to him than just a shag.

In the unlikely event of a man reciprocating a woman's stare, it means he is keen and can see longevity in the friendship, and this is usually how some relationships develop quicker than others.

WHAT TO LOOK OUT FOR!

So we've established that eye contact is nice for her, but uncomfortable for you. Here are five other things you could be looking at while she is trying to undress your soul:

(1) The door.

(2) Your watch. If you're not wearing one, draw one on with a pen.

(3) Pretend to be wiping imaginary crumbs from your jumper.

(4) Her chest. Go on, I dare you.

(5) TV. Most bars, pubs and nightclubs have them these days for such life-saving occasions.

If you are bored and have absolutely nothing better to do on a Sunday afternoon, google Jean Paul Sartre's *The Look*. Actually, fuck that, go for a pint. You'll learn much more about yourself that way.

Do you have any parts of your body that express nonverbal leakage? Have a think, you may be unpleasantly surprised.

Here, smell my wrists!

Female body language, as you may or may not have gathered by now, is much more subtle and controlled than a bloke's. Whereas men seem to appear to just flail their arms around as if they have been thrown overboard into a shark-infested sea, girls' body language is much more secretive and subtle. Some of it though, as this one reveals, is just plain weird.

What do you think of when you think of wrists? Not much, right? As body parts go they are quite bland – devoid of interest and expression – much like Donatella Versace. Apparently though, not for a girl. Apparently wrists are really important. Who knew? If a woman shows you, or 'exposes' her wrists it is a massive sign that she really fancies you.

So next time you are out on first date, stop paying attention to what the girl is saying and lock on to what her wrists are doing. Experts in the field (not, I should point out, *a* field) call this body language 'nonverbal leakage'. When a girl leaks nonverbally (oo er!) it means she is unable to control whether she is closed off or open to you. If she wants to let you in, she'll show you her wrists. Of course, it would be much easier if she just said 'I like you'.

WHAT TO LOOK OUT FOR!

Just look at her wrists – are they facing you or are they facing her? Does it look like she is deliberately trying to show them off? Maybe she's proud of them. These are other parts of a woman that display nonverbal leakage that you might not have originally considered: (1) Knees (2) Ankles (3) Armpits (4) Elbows (5) Knuckles.

NO thanks!

Now, the smutty ones among you, probably think we are being rude here. And, in part, we are. But girls use this fantastic piece of body language to fight off severe temptation – whether it's a slice of calorific chocolate cake when she is already stuffed, something she is potentially allergic to or, yes, her desperate husband, boyfriend or partner's plea for carnal eroticism.

One of the most fantastic things about womankind is that they don't do things by half. Girls can't just shake their heads and say no. They have to add a sense of drama to it.

Experts believe that if a woman is offered a piece of chocolate, for example, even though she wants it (badly) she must make out that she doesn't want it so that no one is thinking 'what a pig'. By using this completely dismissive and dramatic gesture it should register to those around her that 'she is being good' and not giving into temptation.

And then, of course, comes the phrase that blokes around the world hear more than any other… 'OH NO! I COULDN'T POSSIBLY…'

WHAT TO LOOK OUT FOR!

Here are a few other things that girls are more than likely to reply 'Oh no, I couldn't…'

(1) After being offered dessert in a restaurant.

(2) After being offered one more glass of wine (after already guzzling a whole bottle) on a first date for fear of coming across as a wino.

(3) Sex with a man she has only just met.

Next time you are out with your partner, look out for this bizarre hand expression and the phrase 'Oh no, I couldn't possibly…'. Watch for the jazz hands. Hilarious.

If a woman displays three out of the five classic telltale signs mentioned right, then you may get a quick fumble before the evening is finished. If you get all five, well, bully for you!

Look at my lips, goddamit!

The licking of the lips, unless you have gone on a date to KFC, is an obvious body 'tell' to let a man know he is going to be getting a snog at the end of the night. Maybe more, who knows?

Body language experts call this type of signal a 'micro gesture' – a subtle reaction that exposes our inner thoughts even if we think we are not displaying any form of emotion. The human brain is quite deceptive like that.

Now, blokes, if a girl likes you, the subtlety of this move is all that counts. If she is lathering her lips and drooling wildly it might be a good idea to check she's not a basset hound. If she isn't, phew, it probably means she's just hungry. A perfect example of this gesture would be blink-and-you-miss-it. It would be so subtle it would appear to be in super slow-mo with her dragging her tongue above her top lip. She wants you to notice, so pay close attention! You will be rewarded if you do…

WHAT TO LOOK OUT FOR!

This is one of the more secretive female body gestures. You've got to be shrewd and quick to get it. So, here are three more extremely subtle gestures a woman will display to help you out. The question is, will you notice?

(1) She laughs at your jokes – except the one about the woman and the dog.

(2) She talks personally about how cool she is.

(3) She uses 'we' a lot – as in 'Bowling? I love it. We should go!'.

Let's ditch these losers!

Girls can be complex beasts. They may look like they are interested in what you are saying (especially when it's football, they *love* that) but deep down they are thinking of a million ways to ditch you, and your mates, and go and find more interesting men to talk to if you are out in a pub.

The trick here is to look out for the visual signals that women display to one another to suggest they are bored and want to move on. If you start seeing these signs it's up to you to change tack and insert some interest into the conversation – maybe talk about them and what they do for a change?

Now, some women can be very subtle when they want to leave, maybe bump elbows casually, others will just make up blatant excuses such as 'I have to go now' without explaining where to. On the whole though most girls aren't even that nice, most of them will be as cruel as possible to let you know that not only have you bored them rigid, but you've also buzzkilled the last half an hour of their evening. So, if you see girls displaying this ear tug, then you'd better do something spectacular to win them back.

WHAT TO LOOK OUT FOR!

Here are three really interesting facts to mention to a girl if you are having trouble keeping the conversation afloat. Trust us, they never fail: (1) ***Did You Know*** *Donald Duck comics were banned in Finland because he doesn't wear pants? (2)* ***Did You Know*** *It is impossible to lick your elbow? (3)* ***Did You Know*** *The cigarette lighter was invented before the match?*

Here are a few of the classic excuses girls might use on you, if they want to go and talk to other men besides you:

(1) Wow, is that the time? I said I'd meet Jenny at the door at 8.

(2) We're just off to the toilet, back in a minute...

(3) Oh, there's my BOYFRIEND (while pointing to no one) see you guys later MAYBE...

WARNING! Don't start touching a woman until you have written permission to do so from her parents or legal guardian. Best to be safe.

You're in luck!

Body language experts always bang on about how, when flirting with a girl, touching 'breaks the conversation barrier' and that men should only do it after a woman has initiated it. Of course, if the woman feels the date is going particularly well then she may wish to initiate this earlier than the bloke may have expected. WARNING: Some girls are more naturally flirtatious than others and may have their hands all over you but with no intention of going any further. These are called 'mixed signals' and get men into a lot of hot water, needlessly. Some girls will know they are sending out mixed messages just to fuck with a man's head – the poor guy thinking he has secured a lay for the evening may be horrified, come the end, to find out she wasn't that interested. These are exceptional circumstances, but we feel we must warn you now.

If, halfway through chatting a girl up, she starts touching you up – maybe somewhere innocuous first, like your legs – quickly double check later on to make sure she isn't like that with every guy. Perhaps leave her briefly, spy on her, and then come back. This is the only way you'll know if she is genuinely interested in you or not.

WHAT TO LOOK OUT FOR!

If she's touching you, she likes you. Here are five areas she'll touch if she's keen to let you know that you interest her:

(1) Your shoulders (2) Your arms (3) Your back (4) Your hair (5) Basically, anywhere other than your groin (if it's a crowded place). The pub that is, not your groin.

EUGH! YOU PIG!

Some men are idiots. Sorry, most men are idiots. Most men will usually say the most inappropriate thing at the most inappropriate time. It's not like they mean to, it's just that they don't know how to stop themselves. They try and blame the drink, but really it's their genetics. During these situations the brain is screaming out 'GO ON I DARE YA!' while the heart is sobbing 'oh, bloody hell, not again'.

In social situations, maybe after a few drinks, certain types of men will say the wrong thing and end up getting a slap around the face. This is a very easy piece of body language to understand – it means you've been a male chauvinistic pig and you deserve all you get. If you are out in a pub, a man being slapped for his drunken misbehaviour will always elicit a large cheer from the rest of the crowd. Just like the idiots who cheer when somebody breaks a glass, without realising it's probably landed on someone's head. So, to summarise, if you ever see a woman brandishing this nifty bit of body language, you can bet that a man is nearby with a very red face. And he's not blushing.

WHAT TO LOOK OUT FOR!

There are certain 'buttons' a man should never press on a woman. For your safety, here are five of them:

(1) Don't ever call them fat. Ever (2) Don't ever call them 'sugar tits'. Look what happened to Mel Gibson (3) Don't ever try and pick a fight with their boyfriend, no matter how much you think you could 'take him' (4) Don't ever call her a slag, just because she rejected your advances (5) Don't ever tell her that she looks like a man.

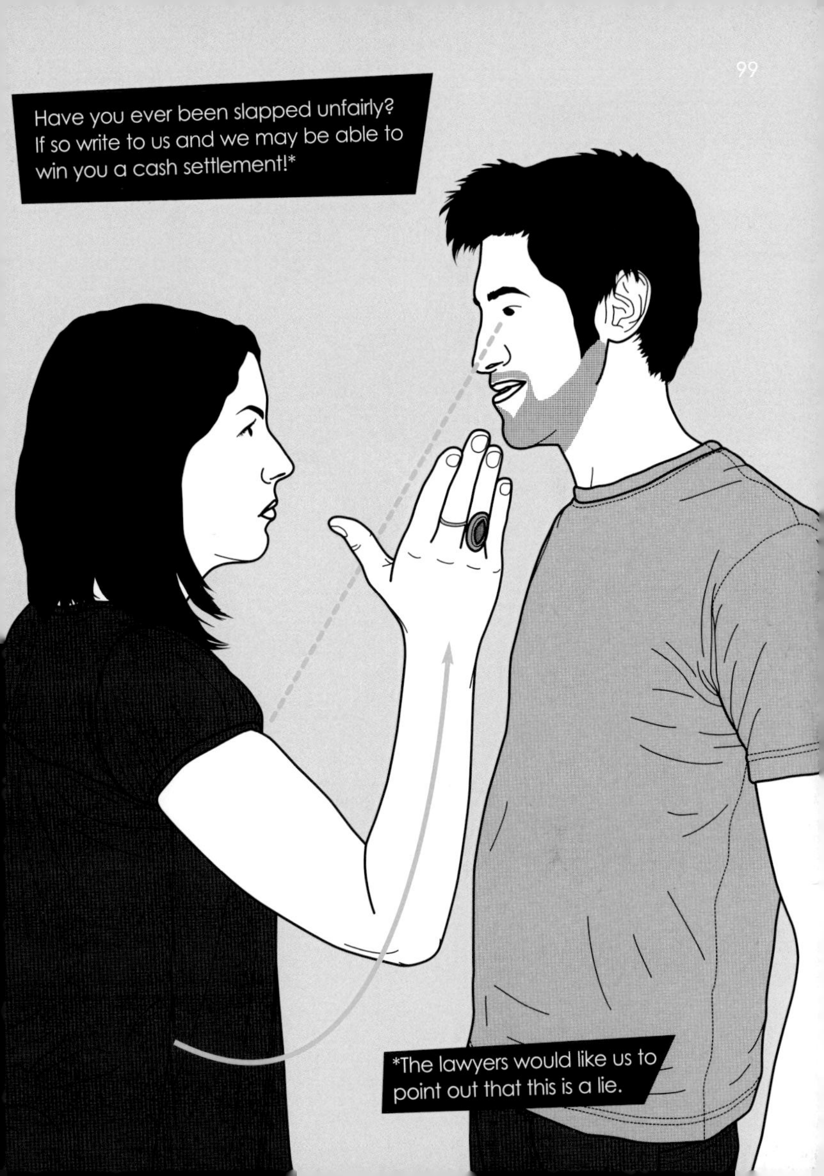
Have you ever been slapped unfairly? If so write to us and we may be able to win you a cash settlement!*
*The lawyers would like us to point out that this is a lie.

Did you know that the only animals on planet Earth that suck their thumbs are humans and chimps? Actually, that's not much of a fact, is it? Dogs, just for the record, can't.

Mummy!

One of the very earliest body language positions human beings learn from inside the womb, and also one of the most obvious body language actions that can accurately portray how a woman feels. It is a gesture that suggests security, comfort and protection. If you see a girl, or even an elderly lady, sucking her thumb it usually means they are uncomfortable or worried and require something comforting to lull them back into feeling secure – just like they did when they felt protected inside their mother as a baby.

Now, many grown women still suck their thumb out of force of habit – maybe they never grew out of it – it is, after all, a 'non-functional motor behaviour' (thanks, wiki). So if you see a woman sucking her thumb, perhaps a woman you have been dating for a few weeks and have only just noticed, don't be alarmed, it could just be a 'sucking reflex' that they continued as they grew up. Doctors call this stereotypic movement disorder (thanks again, wiki).

Thumb-sucking creates strong soothing feelings and makes the sucker feel better so it's probably best if you don't tease, insult or mock her for doing it. Best thing to do if you see her doing it is to throw her some cheeky innuendo, and see if she bites.

WHAT TO LOOK OUT FOR!

Check to see if the girl feels uncomfortable or scared. If a girl starts sucking her thumb, ask yourself these three questions:

(1) Are you watching a scary movie? (2) Are we lost on a deserted motorway about to run out of petrol? (3) Has she just cut her thumb?

Leave me alone!

Ah, yes, the back turn. If you have never experienced a woman turning her back on you, don't worry, you will.

Blokes, when in a sulk, tend to storm off, slamming doors, clumping feet, you know, really make a big deal out of it. Women tend to be more discreet, more subtle, quiet. Why? Because they know the one thing a man can't stand is silence. Men don't understand silence. Men need to fill the air with something, whether it's body gas or conversation about football. If a bloke is in a mood with another bloke they don't sit there in silence, they talk bullshit, they talk about anything at all that isn't their feelings. When a woman sulks at a man, she knows the most effective way to get him to apologise is to say nothing at all – let the man stew in his own juices.

So this classic body language pose, often seen between a quarrelling couple, is well known to blokes around the world and usually ends up with a man muttering 'sod this for a game of soldiers.'

The folded arms are another female defence mechanism to suggest they are closed off from the male, with the slumped shoulders demonstrating they are deflated by the situation.

At this point, men are usually halfway to the pub.

WHAT TO LOOK OUT FOR!

Here are five things not to do to exacerbate this already desperate situation while her back is turned;

(1) Steal money from her purse (2) Start tickling her (3) Creep out the door (4) Give her the two finger salute (5) Massage her shoulders and tell her to 'calm down'.

How do you resolve this situation? Buggered if we know. Answers on a postcard…

Spreading peace is rubbish, as all you are spreading is laziness. Penicillin wasn't discovered by a lazy hippie, it was discovered by a hard-working scientist. But then it wasn't discovered on purpose, It was more of an accident, really. Hmm... you can see the conundrum.

Peace, maaan!

The 1960s were a troubled time. Middle-class people, and mega-rich rock stars who didn't need to work, were out in fields smoking dope and talking about peace, love and gravy. The rest of the country – the working classes and businessmen – still had to go to work for a living and keep the British economy thriving. The booming hippie culture promoted laziness and while 'Sticking It To The Man' sounds like a lot of fun, it's actually quite boring. The greedy, slimy yuppie culture of the 1980s was a direct response to the lack of discipline brought on by the 1960s. All the 1960s demonstrated in the end was that human beings don't want peace, love and happiness. They want money, fame and material possessions. That's why the 1960s only lasted five years and the 1980s vibe is still going strong.

The peace sign is basically a backwards fuck you, which is apt as that's exactly what it is. The peace sign represents sticking two fingers up to The Man, but in a nonviolent, peaceful way. If you see one of those bohemian, hippie chicks flashing the peace sign, resist the urge to tell them the 1960s are over and get a proper job as they are probably too stoned to care.

WHAT TO LOOK OUT FOR!

The peace sign is usually flashed at red-carpet events by peace-loving, environmentalist celebrities. And that's fine, except they probably became famous playing violent action heroes who killed people with a dirty spoon and now drive around in Hummers that drain entire cities of oxygen.

Is that me?

Girls are very conscious of smells. It's one of the main differences that distinguishes them from men. Men are unconcerned by bad odour, in fact, they can be proud of it. If a man works up a massive sweat (say, by doing the crossword) he'll be proud of his manly smell. Likewise, farting among men can cause hilarity and pride if the smell is beyond disgusting. No man is impressed by a small fart…but drop a big hairy one, and everyone will applaud like monkeys.

But for girls, the less smell the better. Some women are incredibly conscious of body odour, choosing to carry their own special brand of deodorant around in their bags. This deodorant, of course, doesn't smell of *anything*. It is odourless, women preferring to smell of Calvin Klein than Sure. Blokes don't care – they will quite happily gas a train full of people with a whole can of Lynx that is uniquely formulated to smell like a jungle or somewhere exotic. We are still waiting for Lynx Bournemouth.

Anyway, for any woman checking her armpits, the resulting body language is a two-tiered motion – the arm lift followed by the armpit sniff, then finished off by the pulling of the top round to make sure there are no stains.

WHAT TO LOOK OUT FOR!

Upon entering any bar, a girl – who had perhaps previously been on a packed train or to the gym – will check underneath her arms for any evidence of residue. Whatever you do don't shout out this:

'Can anyone in here smell shit?'

This is quite a visual sign and very easy to spot. But remember that, on no occasion whatsoever, should you ever point out a woman's sweaty armpits.

Most men and women, at one (or more) points of their lives have done the Walk of Shame. Next time you see someone walk down this path, notice their uncomfortable body language – all contorted and twisted and looking as if they wished they were dead. Which, inside, they may well be.

Am I going red?

Shame. It's a perfectly natural emotion. Young or old, the feeling of shame and embarrassment never leaves you. Everybody remembers that feeling of embarrassment when asking someone out and then being rejected publicly or that time you called your teacher 'mum'. We've all done it. All blokes experience the same feelings, and are no better at dealing with it than girls are. The brain will use body language as a way to defend itself against this unwanted embarrassment.

In body language, hands and arms have a life of their own. They act quickly on instructions from the brain. When you are embarrassed, the brain instructs the hands to cover up the area of the body that is displaying this shame, so as to conceal it, whether your pants have just been pulled down at a party or your trunks have just slid off after diving into the pool. Of course, by then it's too late. But the hands try to spare your blushes. And covering up your reddening face, or naked flesh, only serves to bring more attention to it.

If a girl is alone and no one noticed the incident, she'll just blush. But if she's among friends, and has just embarrassed herself in a very public setting you'll definitely see her clap her hands to her face while uttering these immortal words: 'Am I going red?'

WHAT TO LOOK OUT FOR!

Seeing red? Maybe she's just done one of the following:

(1) Spilled a drink down down her top five minutes after arriving in the pub (2) Just called a guy she fancied at the gym 'dad' (3) Said the word 'dildo' by accident in a work meeting.

Look at my puppies

Some girls have no shame. They aren't ashamed of their bodies. Some girls are especially proud of their bosom and show it off in order to score free drinks and get the undivided attention of every man in the place. In theory these are women to be celebrated and put on a very high pedestal for all womankind to aspire to. Sadly, however, the girls that do get their pups out are usually a) the ones who shouldn't and b) lack any degree of personality.

All of these may be correct, but from a body language perspective – and this is a genuine body language posture – women who display their chests are strong, confident people who are not scared of their sexuality. So if you see a woman walking through a bar with her head held high, chest out, shoulders back and top shirt buttons undone, don't just sit there and gawp, go up to her and commend her on her massive, er, achievement. Because, after all, she wouldn't have them out if she didn't want you to notice them, would she?

WHAT TO LOOK OUT FOR!

If you see a woman with the following it means she wants you to look at her chest:

(1) Tight clothing – this reinforces the shape of the bosom (2) If she is using her arms to physically push up her boobs – to simulate firmness – e.g. at a bar so the barman has no choice but to look down her deep cleavage (3) Undone buttons. One is enough to tease and tantalise and work men up into a lather. Any more than that and it's a free-for-all peep show.

DID YOU KNOW?

Women who display cleavage are subconsciously triggering the sexual connection in men so that it prepares them for thinking about sex, and are therefore ready to mate. If all women went round all tightly trussed up as nuns, men would never think about sex. Unless you liked nuns.

Woman love to talk, so don't be surprised if during a brief pause in your own conversation, she starts to talk and try and swing the subject around to her.

I am listening!

One of the most recognisable body language gestures – and a dead giveaway too, if you suspect your lady is not listening to a bloody word you are saying. Or, even worse, is listening, but is only waiting for a gap in your speech so she can interject with her own opinion, as is her want. Don't you just hate that? When people don't really listen to you, they are just waiting for their turn to speak. It drives us up the wall.

Well, now, by following our advice, you'll know if your girlfriend is genuinely listening or not. Have a look at the illustration on the opposite page. Is this something you see a lot from the lady in your life? Does she often look at you, nodding her head, while at the same time covering her mouth? If so, tell her to stop, because now you know that she just wants to talk. The experts reckon this hand signal is a way people physically try to inhibit themselves from saying something. Maybe they have something interesting and valid to say? Or maybe they are just fucking bored and want to talk about something else, something them-related. Maybe you bore them and they are hiding yawns? Next time you see it happening, ask them…

WHAT TO LOOK OUT FOR!

If a woman is covering her mouth as you are talking, stop and ask if she wants to say something. If she says she doesn't, it's a lie. Not us, her. Maybe change the subject and start talking about these three things: they might pique her interest…

(1) How her day was? (2) What are her plans for the weekend? (3) Is that a new top?

He's soooo cute

The Head Tilt is the first sign a man will recognise in a woman if he thinks she likes him. If she tilts her head, it means she's keen, interested and, above all, fantasising about what he'd look like down the end of the aisle or playing on the swings with her unborn children – the tilt implying she has drifted off into some wondrous pleasure-land of dreamy unreality. She is not, and I repeat this, she is not fantasising about what he'd look like grinding sweatily on top of her.

The head tilt is one of the main ways the brain will differentiate itself from knowing it's flirting and not just boring old talking or listening. If you suddenly catch yourself tilting your head, it's because you've stopped listening and wandered off mentally.

This head tilt happens because the brain is not remaining focused on one particular thought, the head muscles switch off and the head lapses to one side. Dogs also do this when they are looking at their masters puzzled.

WHAT TO LOOK OUT FOR!

In girls, if they are dreaming of how dreamy you happen to be, other subconscious signs will be:

(1) Eyes will flutter madly – this is a massive sign they are into you (or have something massive in their eye) (2) Skin will blush (3) Their hands will be touching their hearts – just like they do in those soppy movies (4) They will take bigger intakes of oxygen, with bigger sighs, sometimes letting out 'mmm' noises as they do – a sign of contentment.

Girls are notoriously sappy creatures. Here are five ways a girl will tell her friends about what she thinks you look like:
(1) Dreamy
(2) Hunky
(3) Lush
(4) Gorgeous
(5) Dishy (oldies only)

And here are five ways a bloke, will probably describe a girl he fancies in a bar:
(1) Fit
(2) Niiiiice!
(3) Oh, yeah, do-able
(4) 9 out of 10, definitely
(5) She'll do

Stan Laurel, the idiot from Laurel and Hardy, was famous for this iconic bit of body language. He would nonverbalise his confusion, and sheer incompetence, by scratching his head – something, you can tell, that really got on Hardy's tits.

I'm not sure

The Head Scratch – nature's way of telling a bloke to get lost. As body language goes, nothing is clearer than the head scratch. Despite its seemingly vague and confusing hand manoeuvring, the head scratch is actually one of the most direct ways a girl can display her emotions.

The scratching of the head means she is not sure. If she is not sure, she'll probably err on the side of saying 'no' if you asked her out. So, if you ask her out, and she scratches her head, consider her a lost cause – move on to one of her friends.

This gesture is the hand's way of motioning the brain into action, to make a decision. Because of the placement of the hand on top of the head, the woman is forcing herself to think about making a decision. Of course, if she has to think about it, the answer is usually negative.

WHAT TO LOOK OUT FOR!

The head scratch is a woman's brain's way of letting you know it's struggling with making a decision. Help it along by saying the three following things:

(1) Can I buy a double shot of tequila for you and your friends?

(2) Has anyone ever told you that you have really nice skin? It's really good…I can tell you must look after yourself.

(3) Did I forget to mention that I am very wealthy? I mean, incredibly, beyond-stupid wealthy?

Kiss my arse!

Women do like to show their bottoms. Whether it's in tight jeans to deliberately reflect the curves of their body or strutting when they walk, bottom-showing is high on a girl's agenda when preparing for a night out on the tiles.

In 2009 President Barack Obama was caught publicly eyeing up a bottom that belonged to a lady that wasn't his wife. This drew massive attention from the media, half disgusted at his wandering eyes, half thinking that it was brilliant that Obama is just a pervert like the rest of mankind.

Some ladies, when annoyed, angered or flustered, ask men to take notice of their behinds in a less romantic expression. Woman want men to kiss their backsides, but get this, ironically. They don't want you to actually kiss it, they want you to do the exact opposite of the literal meaning.

The phrase 'kiss my arse' (or 'ass' if American) is a common dismissive expression of telling someone to piss off, get lost, jog on. The dramatic body language that accompanies this phrase is hysterical, see right…

WHAT TO LOOK OUT FOR!

Being told to 'kiss my arse'? There's probably a good reason for it. Most common reasons why a girl would perform this action are:

(1) A man is shouting rudely at her that she has 'big cans' walking down the street (2) She is replying to her mother's warning to come home before an 11pm curfew (3) Letting her friends know she is exasperated at something they just told her.

Usually after telling someone to 'kiss her arse', a woman will give her behind a little slap just like those people from those annoying ASDA adverts. This is basically to reinforce the statement. A woman may also make raspberry noises to accompany the bending-over action.

Nobody uses cheques anymore so it will be interesting to see what body language human beings will come up with next to reflect the new Chip and Pin technology that everyone is talking about. We suggest tapping numbers into the palm of your hand. Try it out, see if it works, let's start the revolution now!

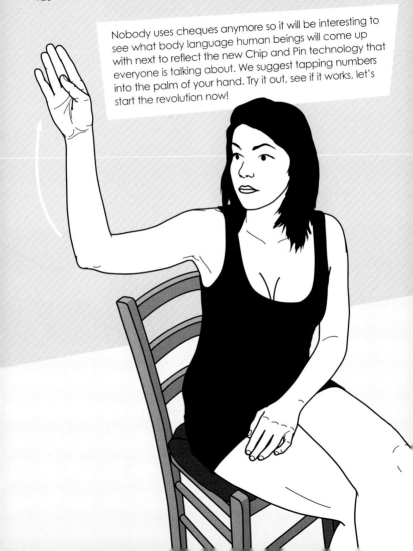

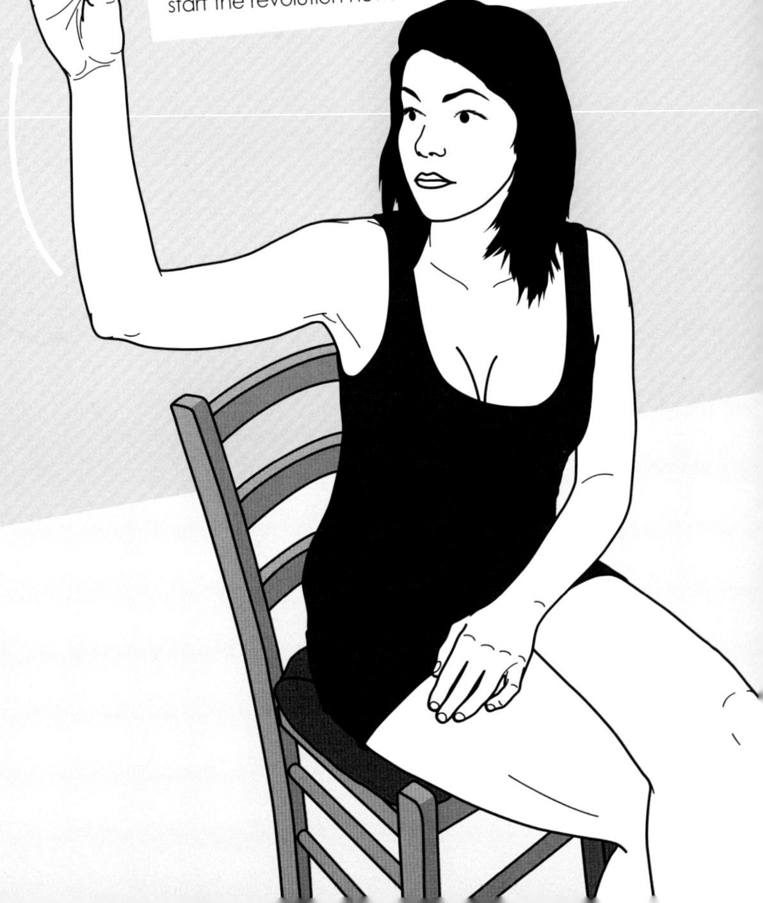

Bill please!

In the olden days (i.e. 5 years ago) men used to say 'cheque please' as a way of signalling to the *garçon*, or waiter if you are stupid and don't understand basic French, that the meal is is finished and they wish to pay the bill.

In this modern era of double-dutching – and because male chivalry is absolutely dead – both women and men now split the bill, especially on the first few dates when both parties are unsure of how they feel about each other. Of course, if a man really likes a girl, he'll pick up the tab. If he wants to sleep with her, he'll definitely pick up the tab. If he's not so keen on her, he'll quite happily let the girl pay for her half and pretend that he's not being a chauvinistic pig, when really he is.

Women, of course, do not mind paying half of the bill. They worked hard for sexual equality and this is one of the perks. These are modern days when sexual equality means that men no longer have to keep doors open for girls (even if he wants to) and woman no longer feel they have to sleep with men just so that they don't turn into sad spinsters like in the 1940s.

WHAT TO LOOK OUT FOR!

This fun expression of direct nonverbal hand gesturing, unthinkable to be used by a woman thirty years ago, is now common and can often be seen by a woman taking a man out to crowded bars promptly before… (1) Firing them (2) Dumping them (3) Firing and dumping them (if it was an office affair).

You twat!

A simple and direct insult – perfect for telling men that they are being idiots and need to 'jog on' – the middle finger insult is one of the few times that a woman can show masculine aggression in her body language.

Body language experts believe that women who display this type of gesture are mirroring the phallic-waving gestures of men who, of course, use their penises as a way of expressing insult – be it literally (the crotch grab), verbally ('you are a dick') or metaphorically ('stop acting like a dick').

The straight finger, in this particular manoeuvre, represents the stiffness of an erect penis. Though if a man attempted to counter this by representing it for real, he'd be locked up in jail.

Giving 'the finger' is a beloved piece of body language – admired in western civilisations for its bluntness and directness and because westerners are totally lazy. Why bother speaking when one finger will do the trick.

WHAT TO LOOK OUT FOR!

Being rejected by a girl, especially by the finger, can be a cruel and unforgiving life lesson. Here are five other things a girl can do with their hands to express themselves:

(1) Thumbs up (e.g. to appreciate) (2) A finger point (e.g. to blame) (3) A fist (e.g. to punch) (4) An palm facing outward (e.g. to suggest 'I've had enough') (5) Fingers crossed (e.g. to pray for a better boyfriend).

The hands, and in particular the fingers are the most expressive part of the body except for the face. One finger alone can express this many emotions: acknowledgement, confidence, defensiveness, dominance, excitement, flirtation, possession, relaxation, sex, stress and disinterest. Without fingers, hands would be pretty boring, wouldn't they?

About the authors

Mal Croft

Mal is a 25-30YO W P M with a GSOH, NS, SD who has NBM and is in a LTR. He is ISO a BI HWP M or F with GSOH for FTA. He is DDF. Well, DF.

He lives and works in London and enjoys dunking ginger nuts.

Matt Windsor

Matt is a Fun Loving NSNDSWMISONSNDSWF25-30YO.

He lives and works in Leighton Buzzard (which sounds much more fun than it is) and frequently pets wild animals even though his mum has told him repeatedly not to.

THANKS:

Phillippa Ann Noaheen Doerr and Miranda Hastings who kindly modelled for the illustrations. Thanks also to Matthew Doerr for letting Matt Windsor photograph both his sister and his girlfriend and despite what they say I did not behave indecently.

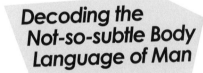